I alone cannot change the world, but I can cast a stone across the waters to create many ripples
Mother   Teresa

Index

What is this book?

If you want to change the world, pick up your pen and write. – Martin Luther King, Jr.

What is this book? In a nutshell it's a rally call from the frontline for much needed change and reform on a number of issues in the United Kingdom today.

My name is Karl and I am in recovery from drink and substance issues. I have been abstinent since 20th February 2015. As well as issues with drink and drugs I have also suffered from mental health issues and at times have developed behavioural addictions such as sex, eating and gambling. My battle is still very much a daily one, if you wish to, you can find out more in depth detail about it in my previous book called 'Get that Monkey off my Back'.

I by no means, claim to have the answers or solutions, but as a human being I am entitled to my own opinions and views of which will be detailed in this book. Some of the ideas are more radical then others and you might find yourselves disagreeing with a lot of what I say, but hopefully some of my views and ideas will make you think and debate just how effective they could be.

The ideas are about a number of issues and subjects right the way from the legal status of drugs and the war on drugs, right the way up to an invention idea I have had to try and reduce drink driving.

On the whole my ideas might be over looked and ignored but my inspiration for writing this book is a guy I read about called Bud Osborn. In a nutshell Bud Osborn was a homeless street addict living on the streets of Vancouver, Canada. Bud was a drug user and had many friends living on the streets who were also dependent on drugs. To avoid punishment for drug taking from the law these people would shoot up drugs in dark spots, behind bins in darkened alley ways. There discretion was ensured but at the cost of there own lives, as if you are hidden away and then you overdose, no one can see you to save you. Bud decided something needed to be done about this and started with his fellow street addicts to patrol the alleyways to try and be there at the point of overdose to save lives by calling for help etc. It worked and overdose death rates dropped rapidly. At this point Bud decided to explore what else he and his team could do, and they started bridging the gap between the street addicts and the communities around them in terms of opinions and stigma, by running street cleaning patrols where, for example they would clean dirty alleyways of used needles etc. One day when in a library Bud learned about a town in Switzerland where they had opened a safe injection site. This was a place where addicts could safely use drugs with clean needles and medical assistance to prevent overdose deaths, as well as being able to connect to services to help them kick the habit and rebuild their lives. Bud decided that this is what was needed in his town. The mayor of the town at the time had an old fashioned view point of addicts and homeless people and his opinion was that addicts should be taken to local detention centers and shot. For about 2 years Bud and his team followed this leader to all events and meetings that he had, protesting, making a racket and even carrying a coffin with a message on it saying something along the lines of 'how many more addicts need to die'. By enlarge Bud and his team was ignored, until after about 2 years this leader decides to see what all the noise is about. He goes undercover on the streets to see what is going on. To his horror he discovers the true extent of the problem and returns to his office with a much refreshed view point. Soon after this guy holds a press conference and he brings one of the addicts up onto the stage with him. He explains that from now on when ever he speaks about issues surrounding addiction, homelessness and mental health he will have one of the addicts by his side to represent the struggling man on the street, and that from now on his town will have a more understanding and compassionate approach to addiction and homelessness, starting with the opening of the towns, and in fact North Americas first safe injection site. Bud was a homeless street addict, probably the most powerless guy you could envisage, yet through sheer passion and persistence he made a change that would go on to resonate world wide, this shows just how much is possible with passion, hard work and persistence.

In terms of the 'war on drugs' Great Britain is stuck in the dark ages, imposed by pre-historic views and outdated systems that no longer work. A Modern country recently named the third best in the world, should be wise enough to look at the examples of other countries such as Portugal and Canada (who were voted ahead of the UK in second spot) and realise that there is another way, a more successful way.

A tiny change today brings a dramatically different tomorrow. – Richard Bach

The Legal status of Cannabis

If you can dream it, then you can achieve it. You will get all you want in life if you help enough other people get what they want. Zig Ziglar

Legalising the sale of cannabis could raise £1 billion a year in tax and help minimise health risks, according to a report. The study, commissioned by the Liberal Democrats and conducted by a panel of scientists, academics and police chiefs, suggests that the drug should be available in specialist shops to over-18s. The party is expected to debate the issue at its spring conference 2016.

Every year billions of pounds are put into the pockets of organised criminals selling cannabis and vast amounts of police time and resources are wasted going after those using the drug. Prohibition of cannabis has failed. It is a waste of police time to go after young people using cannabis and ludicrous to saddle them with criminal convictions that can damage their future careers. A legal market would allow us to have more control over what is sold, and raise a considerable amount in taxation.

The reality is that millions of people use cannabis in the UK and there is a pressing need for government to take control of the trade from gangsters and unregulated dealers. Legal regulation is now working well, despite the fear-mongering, in Colorado and Washington and will roll out across the US over the coming years. This is no longer a theoretical debate and the emerging evidence is only pointing in one direction.

Weed is 114 times safer than alcohol. Cannabis could actually be the safest drug available, after a study found it is actually 114 times less deadly than alcohol, according to the journal, Scientific Reports.
The report studied the effects of alcohol, heroin, cocaine, tobacco, ecstasy, crystal meth and cannabis.

Surprise! Legalising weed doesn't cause a crime epidemic. Despite the predictions of right wing politicians, in Colorado, which legalised recreational use of marijuana, there has been no epidemic of crime. Overall, crime has fallen by 15% and murder has dropped by 50%.

Weed can kill cancer cells. Marijuana can kill cancer cells, the US government have confirmed, and can also shrink some of the most serious types of brain tumors. The research was carried out by the National Institute on Drug Abuse. Some believe cannabis oil can 'cure' cancer. A cancer patient claims to have been cured by cannabis. A cancer patient had been told he only had 18 months to live but now he's looking forward to life with his new bride after being given the all clear. The 33-year-old, from Stoke-on-Trent, Staffordshire, said this miraculous turn of events was down to him taking cannabis oil, which cost £50 a gram from a local dealer.

Weed is actually less addictive than drinking coffee. Coffee's addictive effects mean that it might actually be a more harmful drug than weed, an expert has argued. Caffeine ticks off just as many boxes as for drug abuse as THC, the active ingredient in cannabis.

Legalising weed would recharge the British economy. If we legalised cannabis, up to £1 billion could be raised annually in taxes, according to the Institute for Economic Research.
States such as Colorado which have legalised cannabis have seen increased tax revenues.

Most people now believe smoking weed is safe and no longer worry that a puff on a joint will either kill them, or turn them into a murdering psychopath. There has been a MASSIVE shift in public opinion in the past decade – in 2002, a majority of people believed that there were large risks attached to smoking weed once or twice a week. That figure has now dropped from 51% to 40% in America, according to data from the National Survey on Drug Use and Health.

Legalising weed creates jobs. In American states such as Colorado, where cannabis has been legalised, thousands of jobs have been created. Ten thousand people now work in the area's cannabis industry.

Legalising weed DOESN'T encourage young people to smoke it. In Colorado, legalising cannabis has actually led to a drop in the number of young people smoking it.

Most people in the UK and the U.S. now support weed being legalised. As states in America have legalised weed without society breaking down, people's attitudes to it have softened. In both America and Britain, opinion polls show that a majority of people support weed being legalised, it's just political parties who don't.

The pros and cons of legalising drugs.

Pro: The war on drugs creates addicts.
Russell Brand, Sir Richard Branson, Sting and Michael Mansfield QC were among high-profile signatories to an open letter asking David Cameron to consider decriminalising possession of cannabis. Cannabis has been classified as a Class B drug in the UK since 2008 and carries a prison sentence of up to five years for possession. Release, the drugs charity which organised the letter, says arresting users "creates more harm for individuals, their families and society". It says that if users are not "caught up in the criminal justice system" they have a better chance of escaping addiction and argues that evidence from other countries supports this view. According to Release, users of 'soft' drugs like cannabis are more likely to try something harder, including heroin, when both are illegal.

Con: Legalising drugs would create addicts.
A leading US academic and opponent of drug liberalisation, said last year: "Legal regulation has been a disaster for drugs like alcohol and tobacco. Both of those drugs are now sold by highly commercialised industries that thrive off addiction for profit". He concluded: "What we need is much smarter law-enforcement, coupled with real demand reduction in places like Europe and the US". At a time when governments are uniting to stop people smoking, should they really be becoming more laissez-faire about drug use?

Pro: If you can't beat them, regulate them.
Sir William Patey, the former UK ambassador to Afghanistan, ruffled feathers last year when he came out in favor of legalising the trade in opium poppies, from which heroin is derived. Writing in The Guardian, Patey said it was impossible to stop Afghan farmers from growing and exporting opium illegally, and concluded that "if we cannot deal effectively with supply" the only alternative is to "limit the demand for illicit drugs by making a licit supply of them available from a legally-regulated market". This would create stability and peace in drug-producing nations.

Con: Regulation may overstep the mark.
The Misuse of Drugs Act of 1971 classifies drugs as illegal in the UK based on their chemical compounds. The European Monitoring Centre for Drugs and Drug Addiction says that, due to small alterations in the chemical formulae of illegal drugs, two new legal highs are discovered in Europe every week. In an effort to combat this trend, ministers have introduced a law banning all psychoactive substances, which could technically cover everything from hot chocolate to heroine. Notably, caffeine, food and nicotine are

exempt. Among the proposed banned substances are drugs that have been legally sold and used in the UK for decades, such as laughing gas and poppers.

Pro: Ganja is good for business
In Jamaica, one of the major arguments in favor of decriminalising ganja, as cannabis is known there, was an economic one. As well as making possession less dangerous (it currently only results in a fine), the government has now legalised growing for medical purposes. The island hopes for a gold-rush selling the drug to US states which allow its therapeutic use, says the Daily Telegraph. Even the US State Department acknowledges that Jamaica is the largest Caribbean supplier of marijuana to the United States.

Con: The Pope wouldn't like it
Pope Francis has tarnished his glowing liberal credentials as the tweeting pontiff who spoke inclusively about gay people, denounced "unbridled capitalism" and reached out to Muslims, by speaking out against decriminalisation. Francis is a native of Argentina, which borders Uruguay where cannabis is now legally grown and smoked. He said legalising recreational drugs was "highly questionable" and would "fail to produce the desired effects", reported the Daily Mail. He added that legalisation was "a veiled means of surrendering to the problem".

Drug laws around the world. Jamaica decriminalised the possession of small amounts of the drug, and in Portugal the possession of small quantities of any drug has been decriminalised. In December 2013, Uruguay became the first nation to make it legal to grow, consume and sell the plant. That said, all sales must pass through a government run marketplace, and the administration has yet to set up that system. Twenty-three US states and the District of Columbia allow marijuana for medical purposes and Washington became the first to permit the recreational use of the plant in 2012, despite a federal ban. Colorado, Oregon, Alaska and the District of Columbia have since followed suit. Cannabis went on sale in Washington in July 2014.

What happened as a result?

The legalisation of cannabis in some US states has not led to a rise in adolescent use, a US study found. It revealed that while cannabis use was generally higher in the states that had passed medical marijuana legislation before 2014, the passage of such laws did not affect the rate of marijuana use in those states.

It is my view that, we should legalise Cannabis. I will speak more in another section in this book about the legalisation of other drugs as well. There should be safe and controlled measures for the use of cannabis by doctors and pharmaceutical companies, given the proven health benefits of cannabis. Furthermore we should open vape and off-license style stores to regulate the safe distribution of safe cannabis onto our streets. In effect we should treat cannabis with the same attitude as alcohol which is actually a lot more of a risk then cannabis, but is fully legal and widely and commercially available 24 hours a day. Regulating cannabis would create over one billion pounds in revenue, a great portion of which should be re-invested into proper treatment services for addiction and rehabilitation facilities and schemes to aid an individual's recovery. This said if bootleggers in the market appear under the radar, which they undoubtedly will, there should be suitable laws in place to prevent this, the same way there is for bootleg alcohol factories.

Some historical users of Cannabis include: William Shakespeare, Queen Victoria, Joan of Arc, Egyptian Pharaohs, George Washington, Queen Elizabeth I, Christopher Columbus, Hua Tuo, Shennong, William Brooke O'Shaughnessy and Barack Obama.

PRINCE Charles is growing opium poppies in his private gardens at Highgrove. The green-fingered prince is said to consider the plants, which are harvested by farmers in Afghanistan to produce heroin, among his favorites in the grounds of his Gloucestershire estate. Named "papaver somniferum", the species is also the source of pharmaceutical drugs including morphine and codeine which are used to treat severe pain. The sap can be extracted, however, and used to make heroin when it is refined and then chemically treated. In the UK the poppies are legal to grow but a licence is needed to use them for medicinal purposes. The plant was listed in the top 24 of HRH's favourite species at Highgrove Gardens, according to Gardening Illustrated magazine. The listing reads: "Injecting a touch of glamour in early summer borders, opium poppies come in a huge range of colours, including this vivid single form, with its dark throat". The list also includes the delphinium black knight group, of which the Prince is said to be "passionate", and the southern marsh orchid, which is threatened in many parts of the country. The private gardens are regarded as among the best cultivated in the country and are only open to the public through guided tours booked months in advance. The Prince has long been known as a gardening enthusiast. His first move when arriving at his retreat near Tetbury, where he took up residence in 1980, is said to be to slip on his outdoor slippers to attend to his oasis. Gardening expert Mike Seaton said: "I can see no problem with it at all. The poppy family has some absolutely stunning varieties, such as Himalayan poppies, and the flowers look great in a garden. Prince Charles is a very keen horticulturalist, so why not? They are pretty harmless." Opium poppies are harvested by pharmaceutical companies in the UK to make pain-relieving drugs including morphine. Papaver somniferum was first harnessed for commercial use on British farms in 2002. Crops are now grown in Dorset, Hampshire, Lincolnshire and Oxfordshire. Traditionally, morphine had been imported but the plants are increasingly being grown in the UK to reduce costs.

Why is marijuana against the law? It grows naturally upon our planet. Doesn't the idea of making nature against the law seem to you a bit . . . unnatural?
— Bill Hicks

Supervised Injecting Rooms

In fact, once he is motivated no one can change more completely than the man who has been at the bottom. I call myself the best example of that. - Malcolm X

Supervised injection rooms are legally sanctioned facilities where people who use intravenous drugs can inject pre obtained drugs under medical supervision. Supervised injection facilities are designed to reduce the health and societal problems associated with injection drug use. These facilities now operate in dozens of cities around the world and have been shown to reduce injection related risks and harms like vein damage, overdose, and transmission of diseases like HIV/AIDS and hepatitis C.

A safe injecting room is a clean, safe, supervised environment where users can inject their own drugs off the streets, and connect to addiction, health care and community services. These sites are supported by a broad range of organisations and individuals. Participants using the supervised injection sites are checked into a database by codenames before injecting, which allows staff to track usage without compromising participants' anonymity.

InSite a safe injecting site in Canada allows participants to access a 12 seat injection room where they can inject their own drugs under the supervision of nurses and trained staff. They have access to clean injection equipment, including syringes, sterile cookers, filters, water and tourniquets. The use of this equipment has been shown to reduce the spread of infectious diseases as well as reduce the number of serious soft tissue infections, which intravenous drug users are susceptible to. After injecting, participants move to a post injection room, where they can have a glass of water and rest until they feel ready to leave the premises. Staff are on hand to help connect participants to other services including primary care for treatment of wounds, abscesses and other infections, addiction counseling and peer support and referral to treatment services such as withdrawal management, opiate replacement and other services. Staff can also refer participants directly to OnSite, a 30-bed detox and treatment program that is co-managed by the PHS Community Services Society and Vancouver Coastal Health, located right above the supervised injection site. Insite is a harm reduction program that is meant to be part of a continuum of care for people with addiction, mental illness and HIV/AIDS. For many injection users, InSite is the first step in the recovery process, the goal being to move participants towards health and addiction services that will keep them alive, and eventually improve their health. Some of the ways that InSite benefits participants and the community:

Connecting participants to programs: InSite engages a marginalised population that is hard to reach through conventional methods, mainly due to their struggles with homelessness, one or more mental illnesses, injection dug addictions and trauma. The non-judgmental environment at Insite helps participants to develop trusting relationships with the staff, which in turn helps the staff connect them to key services and programs that they might not otherwise access.

Limiting the spread of disease: InSite participants have access to clean equipment and education on safe injection practices, which helps limit the spread of diseases such as HIV/Aids and hepatitis C.

Overdose prevention: Participants injecting at InSite are supervised by nurses, who ensure that medical help is immediate should an overdose occur. To date, well over 2400 overdoses have occurred at InSite, with no fatalities.

Increased public order: InSite contributes to increased public order by helping to limit public injections and discarded syringes.

Cost-effective health care: Preventative health measures provided by InSite limiting overdose deaths and the spread of diseases such as HIV/AIDS and hepatitis C saves the health care system over $6 million annually.

The case against safe injecting rooms is quite simple. Every time the addict shoots up it may be his last hit. To provide state sanction for such dangerous activity is irresponsible in the extreme. It is playing Russian roulette with the addict's life. Even earlier advocates stopped calling them 'safe' but 'supervised' injecting rooms. Drugs can never be safely injected, any more than one can safely play with a live hand grenade.

A lightning rod for controversy, Insite attracts support and detractors along several main lines.

Supporters say:

It saves lives:

There have been no overdose deaths at Insite since it opened in 2003. On average, nearly 600 injections occur daily at the site and in one year alone there were more than 200 'overdose interventions' by Insite staff that provides oxygen or drugs to users who are in danger of overdosing. A paper published in the Lancet in also noted that fatal overdoses within 500 metres of Insite decreased by 35 per cent after the facility opened compared to a decrease of nine per cent in the rest of Vancouver.

It serves as a bridge to detox and treatment: Insite was conceived of as part of a four-pillar approach being harm reduction, prevention, treatment and enforcement, modeled on similar programs that jurisdictions such as Switzerland and Germany pursued in the 1990s. By offering a clean, safe, non-judgmental environment to shoot up, the reasoning goes; Insite allows drug users to connect with other services, whether that is treatment for a drug related abscess or dental care. Insite staff makes more than 5,000 referrals to other social and health agencies every year, including 458 admissions to Onsite, a neighboring detox facility that opened in 2007 and recorded a 'program completion rate' of 43 per cent in 2010. Supporters say supervised injection facilities should be seen as just one piece of a bigger puzzle in treating drug addiction and its related toll on society.

It benefits public health and the broader community: Among the many studies published on Insite are papers that conclude the clinic has not led to an increase in drug related crime, is not a negative influence of those seeking to stop drug use and has resulted in a drop in public injections in back alleys and doorways. Studies have also reported declines in dangerous behavior, such as sharing needles, and a related decrease in HIV infections. The Vancouver Police Department supports the facility, which studies have shown has resulted in fewer discarded needles in neighborhood streets.

In fighting to keep Insite open, the provincial government argues that the health benefits of the facility should trump jurisdictional issues, saying in written submissions to the court that British Columbians have a 'visceral' memory of hundreds of addicts dying needlessly in flophouses and on the street before Insite was opened.

Those who want to see the site closed maintain:

Insite's operation is an affront to federal control: When Insite opened; it obtained a three-year exemption from Canada's Controlled Drugs and Substances Act from Health Canada. That exemption was extended twice, until June 30, 2008. When the federal government declined to extend the exemption, Insite supporters launched a court challenge. The B.C. Supreme Court and the B.C. Court of Appeal supported B.C.'s right to run the clinic on health grounds. The federal government appealed. Federal prosecutors say Ottawa needs to maintain control over drug policy and that giving B.C. control over Insite would open the door to a fragmented, patchwork of rules and regulations across the country. The legal wrangle will zero in on the constitutional conundrum posed by Insite, the federal government has authority over criminal law and the promotion of health and safety, but provinces decide how health care can be delivered.

Governments should not facilitate drug use: Despite the research studies backing Insite and its harm-reduction approach, there is still profound discomfort for many with any facility that gives addicts a green light to inject illegal drugs and flout the law. Governments, they argue, should not be facilitating illegal, dangerous activities. "The state has no constitutional obligation to facilitate drug use at a specific location by hardcore addicts, the mildly addicted, frequent users or occasional users," federal prosecutors Robert Frater and W. Paul Riley said in written submissions to the court. There have been arguments that money spent on Insite would be better spent on services such as treatment and that government's support of supervised injection sites sends a mixed message to young people who might be considering illicit drug use.

Supervised injection sites do nothing to deter drug use or help drug addicts: Part of the federal government's argument is that drug laws are not an unreasonable restriction on individuals' liberty. "Unsafe injection or, for that matter, consumption by injection at all, is a choice made by the consumer," the federal prosecutors say in their brief to the Supreme Court. There are also arguments that supervised injection sites are a magnet for drug dealers and predators, and that public safety demands that illegal drugs be tightly controlled.

There are many safe injecting sites already open worldwide and I want to campaign to open some in the UK. I feel we should start of with about half a dozen sites in major cities such as Glasgow, London, Birmingham, Cardiff and also in areas with the worse rates of poverty and drug use in the United Kingdom, such as Blackpool and Hull. I feel the proven benefits of safe injection rooms are enough argument to try this new approach and reduce deaths from overdoses in the United Kingdom.

Every reform movement has a lunatic fringe - Theodore Roosevelt

Portugal

Laws do not persuade just because they threaten. - Seneca, A.D. 65

In 2001, the Portuguese government did something that the United States would find entirely alien. After many years of waging a fierce war on drugs, it decided to flip its strategy entirely: It decriminalised them all.

If someone is found in the possession of less than a ten day supply of anything from marijuana to heroin, he or she is sent to a three person Commission for the Dissuasion of Drug Addiction, typically made up of a lawyer, a doctor and a social worker. The commission recommends treatment or a minor fine; otherwise, the person is sent off without any penalty. A vast majority of the time, there is no penalty.

Fourteen years after decriminalisation, Portugal has not been run into the ground by a nation of drug addicts. In fact, by many measures, it's doing far better than it was before.

The background: In 1974, the dictatorship that had isolated Portugal from the rest of the world for nearly half a century came to an end. The Carnation Revolution was a bloodless military led coup that sparked a tumultuous transition from authoritarianism to democracy and a society wide struggle to define a new Portuguese nation. The newfound freedom led to a raucous attitude of experimentalism toward politics and economy and, as it turned out, hard drugs.

Portugal's dictatorship had insulated it from the drug culture that had swept much of the Western world earlier in the 20th century, but the coup changed everything. After the revolution, Portugal gave up its colonies, and colonists and soldiers returned to the country with a variety of drugs. Borders opened up and travel and exchange were made far easier. Located on the westernmost tip of the continent, the country was a natural gateway for trafficking across the continent. Drug use became part of the culture of liberation, and the use of hard narcotics became popular. Eventually, it got out of hand, and drug use became a crisis.

At first, the government responded to it in a familiar way, a conservative cultural backlash that vilified drug use and a harsh, punitive set of policies led by the criminal justice system. Throughout the 1980s, Portugal used this approach, but to no avail. By 1999, nearly 1% of the population was addicted to heroin, and drug-related AIDS deaths in the country were the highest in the European Union.

By 2001, the country decided to decriminalise possession and the use of drugs, and the results have been remarkable. It is approached much the same way as a parking ticket. As part of its war on drugs, Portugal has stopped prosecuting users. The substances listed in the Law 30/2000 table are still illegal in Portugal otherwise they would have gotten into trouble with the UN, but using these drugs is nothing more than a misdemeanor, much the same as a parking violation.

As a result among Portuguese adults, there are now only 3 drug overdose deaths for every 1,000,000 citizens. Comparable numbers in other countries range from 10.2 per million in the Netherlands to 44.6 per million in the UK, all the way up to 126.8 per million in Estonia. The EU average is 17.3 per million. Perhaps more significantly, the use of 'legal highs' like so called synthetic marijuana, bath salts and the like is lower in Portugal than in any of the other countries for which reliable data exists. This makes a lot of intuitive sense: why bother with fake weed or dangerous designer drugs when you can get the real stuff? This is arguably a positive development for public healths in the sense that many of the designer drugs that people develop to skirt existing drug laws have terrible and often deadly side effects.

I am a massive advocate for what countries like Canada and Portugal have done in recent years in their approach to the war on drugs. These countries have de-criminalised all drugs from crack to weed. Instead they have re-distributed all the money they used on chasing, arresting and prosecuting addicts, and instead put the money into proper treatment for addicts and back to work programs and other schemes to help recovered addicts re-connect with their communities and become valued members of them. If we continue to prosecute addicts and give them criminal records, all it will do is further cut them off from society and outcast them into the endless cycle of addiction. We need to do the opposite; the opposite of addiction is connection. I think given the way other countries have a more modern, realistic and hugely successful approach on how to deal with addicts now, if you are sent to jail and get a criminal record and come back out of prison to being un-employable and having not had proper treatment and help and you feel a huge temptation to re-use because you have little else going for you, then I think you have every right to feel a victim of an old fashioned system and approach that does not work anymore. It is hard enough alone being a victim of the amount of stigma that there still is around addicts in this day and age.

As an investment, the war on drugs has failed to deliver any returns. If it were a business, it would have been shut down a long time ago. This is not what success looks like – Richard Branson

Education

Education is the most powerful weapon which you can use to change the world - Nelson Mandela

One major thing that we need to do is increase the amount of education done on the use and risks of alcohol and substances, especially as early as the 6th year of education which would be around the age of 10 or 11 years old.

I believe that we now live in an age where once kids go to secondary school the chances of experimenting with alcohol and substances especially through peer pressures is a lot more common than it used to be say 10 or 20 years ago. I'm not saying we should go in with a 'just say no' attitude as when kids are that age the more you tell them something is bad and not to do it, the more natural curiosity there will be and cooler it will seem and this will inevitably lead to rebellion. What we should instead do is simply offer the youth of today the facts, figures and case studies, a bit of shock and owe pictures and videos to simply give them the tools to make their own educated decisions on what to do.

We also need to make them aware that if they run into problems there is help available and it is ok to reach out for it. Ensure that they are aware that there is no shame or stigma in reaching out for help. We should offer first aid as well on the basics of if someone overdoses on drugs or develops problems whilst drunk to increase our first line of care and prevent alcohol or drug related injuries or deaths. I would also like to see Naloxone stocked within schools and other youth facilities. I would hope the supply would never need to be used but we must practice a better safe than sorry attitude. A medication called Naloxone can reverse the effects of an overdose of heroin or some types of painkillers. Paramedics and emergency room doctors have used it for years to save lives.

Education is the movement from darkness to light - Allan Bloom

University Education

In a modern first world country like Great Britain, education in all its forms should be a fundamental human right and therefore free. We are punishing people with a life times debt for wanting to better themselves, when we should be doing all we can to encourage the next generation to do more then leave education prematurely and rot away on the dole queue – Karl Newton

As a new full-time student starting your university course from August 2016, the maximum tuition fee you can be charged in the academic year 2016/17 is: £3,925 if you study in Northern Ireland and up to £9,000 if you study elsewhere in the United Kingdom.

England has the highest average undergraduate tuition fees in the industrialised world, although this investment tends to be repaid many times in higher graduate wages, according to an annual survey of education across more than 30 countries. On average, English undergraduates paid just under £6,000 in annual tuition fees in the 2013-14 year, after the government's decision to triple maximum fees, according to the Organisation for Economic Co-operation and Development (OECD). The next highest was the USA, with fees of about £5,300, followed by Japan on about £3,300, said the Paris-based organisation, which comprises 34 mainly prosperous countries. The comparison applies for public universities only, which skews the figures for the US, where many leading universities are private.

Free education enables everyone to have the opportunity to study. This means there would be more people going to universities. The outcome of this would be that in our society, more people will have higher degrees which means would be more people who are doctors, lawyers, nonprofit workers, teachers, business leaders etc. This has positive benefits. More doctors mean more people who treat those who are sick. More teachers' means, better quality of education for students. More nonprofit workers mean more people who are trying to help and raise money for those who need it. When the number of people who get an education rises, the number of people who benefit from that persons education also rises. Therefore, free education will benefit our society because there will be more highly educated individuals who have the education and ability to help others.

"We believe education is a right that should be accessible to everyone and barriers such as fees are unjust," says the National Campaign against Fees and Cuts.

The Green party agrees; their manifesto includes a pledge to abolish tuition fees as well as writing off any outstanding loans. The party has costed this at just over £12bn a year, roughly three times what the government spent on unemployment benefit last year, or more than the entire budget for transport.

There seems to be little appetite among the major parties to make free higher education a reality except from Ukip, who would make Stem subjects free to study.

However Germany recently scrapped its tuition fees, leading some to question why Britain couldn't do the same. Education in most of Europe is already very different from what it is in the USA, Canada, or Australia. In several countries from the Old Continent, most notably Scandinavian countries Sweden, Norway and Denmark education has been free for several years, and other countries are starting to follow suite. Germany is the first in hopefully a long list of countries to completely remove university tuition fees. "Tuition fees are socially unjust," said Dorothee Stapelfeldt, senator for science in Hamburg, which scrapped charges in 2012. "They particularly discourage young people who do not have a traditional academic family background from taking up studies. It is a core task of politics to ensure that young women and men can study to a high quality standard, free of charge in Germany".

Indeed, the general trend seems to be to reduce or eliminate tuition fees for higher education. The notable exception here is Great Britain. With some exceptions like for example Welsh Universities being free for Welsh people, the UK tuition fees are starting to rival those in the US. But it seems more logical to treat higher education like an investment in the country's future, and not like a private company. It seems logical for the government to support higher education from taxes, thus investing in its future.

We keep hearing about things like too many unemployed people or the job market being too competitive in Great Britain. Scrapping university fees is one way to solve these problems. More skilled workers and more people in education being groomed into the society leaders of tomorrow rather then rotting away on the dole line.

I want to see all education fees scrapped, especially the fees applicable to an individual if they wanted to go back into part time education as an adult. Everybody deserves the fundamental right to improve themselves and money shouldn't be a barrier to do so. Instead of discouraging people to better themselves, we should be giving them grants to encourage them to study and better themselves and contribute more to this countries economy.

Education is our passport to the future; for tomorrow belongs to those that prepare for it today – Malcom X

Cuts in all the right places

A bill, by the bye, is the most extraordinary locomotive engine that the genius of man ever produced. It would keep on running during the longest lifetime, without ever once stopping of its own accord – Charles Dickens

In the fiscal year ending in 2015, total UK public spending, including central government and local authorities, was £748 billion. In the fiscal year ending in 2016, total UK public spending is expected to be £760 billion. Investing in public services is the solution to the deficit crisis. Instead of cutting jobs, we should be creating them. Jobs are not created by bullying people on benefits into jobs that don't exist. Instead there are several areas where public sector jobs urgently need to be created.

It has been estimated that over a million 'climate jobs' could be created if the government was serious about tackling both climate change and unemployment – these would include areas like housing, renewable energy and public transport investment including high speed rail, bus networks and electric car manufacture. Today there are 1.8 million families representing over 5 million people on council house waiting lists. There is an urgent need to build affordable housing for these people, which would also help reduce housing benefit payments. The UK lags behind much of the rest of Europe in the development of a high-speed rail network, which would have the potential to create thousands of jobs and reduce carbon emissions by shifting passengers and freight away from road and air travel. Much of the country outside of London also needs huge investment in bus services – and, just as we should invest in electric car technology, we should also invest in electric buses and tram networks. Only 2.2% of UK energy comes from renewable sources compared with 8.9% in Germany, 11% in France, and an impressive 44.4% in Sweden. If we are committed to tackling climate change and ensuring domestic energy security there needs to be investment in renewable energy technology.

All of these industries would generate revenue as people are billed for electricity, buy tickets to travel on public transport, and pay rent for council housing. Research by Richard Murphy of Tax Research has shown that the state recoups 92% of the cost of creating new public sector jobs through lower benefit payments and increased tax revenues.

The Banks. We should never forget that it was the banking sector that caused the recession, and is ultimately responsible for the huge debts that the UK has amassed. Despite causing the crisis, the banking sector has escaped any significant regulation, and bankers are again awarding themselves huge bonuses. As a result of the UK government's £1.3 trillion bailout to the financial sector, the government still owns over £850 billion in bank assets. This figure is roughly equal to the total UK debt. The UK has an 84% stake in RBS and a 41% stake in Lloyds TSB. In addition, the state also owns Northern Rock and Bradford & Bingley. Under public ownership and control these assets could yield significant annual income to the Government, and could be used to meet social needs and tackle financial exclusion.

The case against privatization. As a result of the government's agenda to slash the public sector, privatization, outsourcing and the Private Finance Initiative (PFI) are a fast growing threat to civil and public services despite the many performance failures of past privatisations. Privatization is no solution to the national debt. Evidence confirms that after transfer to the private sector the terms and conditions of workers are worse than before, the public sector loses any revenue stream while ultimately keeping the risk, and services to the public decline or cost more:

In the DWP, welfare is now described as an annual multi-billion pound market, and despite the department's own research showing that Job centre staff outperform the private sector in helping people back to work; all contracts for welfare programmes are now outsourced.

Qinetiq was a company formed from the privatisation of the Defence Evaluation and Research Agency (DERA). In 2007, the 10 most senior managers gained £107.5m on a total investment of £540,000 in the company's shares. The return of 19,990% on their investment was described as "excessive" by the National Audit Office. In 2009, Qinetiq offered its staff a pay freeze.

Although the economic downturn has led to a drying up of bank finance for PFI projects, the government has got round this by funneling public funds through the Treasury's Infrastructure Finance Unit to state owned banks who then loan finance to PFI consortia, which then claim inflated returns to government for the next thirty years, greatly exceeding the money given to them. The journalist and anti-privatisation activist George Monbiot observed, "The Private Finance Initiative no longer requires much private finance or initiative".

Public services were won by trade union struggles in an effort to establish the basis of a civilised society. Driven by the desire for maximum profits, the private sector fails to provide effective and efficient public services.

Tax justice. Addressing the 'tax gap' is a vital part of tackling the deficit. Figures produced for PCS by the Tax Justice Network show that £25 billion is lost annually in tax avoidance and a further £70 billion in tax evasion by large companies and wealthy individuals. An additional £26 billion is going uncollected. Therefore PCS estimates the total annual tax gap at over £120 billion which is more than three-quarters of the annual deficit! It is not just PCS calculating this; leaked Treasury documents in 2006 estimated the tax gap at between £97 and £150 billion.

JP Morgan, Bank of America Merrill Lynch, Deutsche Bank AG, Nomura Holding and Morgan Stanley make billions in profit in Britain – but analysis reveals their UK arms paid not a penny of business levy in 2014. One in four of the UK's top companies pay no tax while we give THEM millions in credits. Global firms such as Starbucks, Google and Amazon have come under fire for avoiding paying tax on their British sales.

High profile celebrities including Katie Melua and George Michael were accused of hypocrisy yesterday for using an aggressive tax avoidance scheme despite preaching the importance of paying their taxes. They are among 1,600 wealthy celebrities, business leaders, lawyers and doctors who together tried to shelter £1.2billion from the taxman via a complicated network of offshore companies. Sir Michael Caine, Gary Barlow and two of his Take That bandmates, BBC presenter Anne Robinson and four members of rock group the Arctic Monkeys also invested in the highly controversial 'Liberty' scheme, a leaked database revealed.

What are the Panama Papers? The files show how Mossack Fonseca clients were able to launder money, dodge sanctions and avoid tax. In one case, the company offered an American millionaire fake ownership records to hide money from the authorities. This is in direct breach of international regulations designed to stop money laundering and tax evasion. It is the biggest leak in history, dwarfing the data released by the Wikileaks organisation in 2010. For context, if the amount of data released by Wikileaks was equivalent to the population of San Francisco, the amount of data released in the Panama Papers is the equivalent to that of India.

Who is in the papers?

There are links to 12 current or former heads of state in the data, including dictators accused of looting their own countries. More than 60 relatives and associates of heads of state and other politicians are also implicated. The files also reveal a suspected billion dollar money laundering ring involving close associates of Russia's President, Vladimir Putin. Also mentioned are the brother-in-law of China's President Xi Jinping; Ukraine President Petro Poroshenko; Argentina President Mauricio Macri; the late father of UK Prime Minister David Cameron and three of the four children of Pakistan's Prime Minister Nawaz Sharif. The documents show that Iceland's Prime Minister, Sigmundur Gunnlaugsson, had an undeclared interest linked to his wife's wealth. He has now resigned. The scandal also touches football's world governing body, Fifa. Part of the documents suggest that a key member of Fifa's ethics committee, Uruguayan lawyer Juan Pedro Damiani, and his firm provided legal assistance for at least seven offshore companies linked to a former Fifa vice-president arrested last May as part of the US inquiry into football corruption.

The basic annual salary for an MP from 1 April 2016 is £74,962. MPs also receive expenses to cover the costs of running an office, employing staff, having somewhere to live in London and in their constituency, and travelling between Parliament and their constituency.

So with all these facts and figures what am I getting at? Well there are a number of things that I want to campaign for or in some cases against, and I guess it all boils down to money, here is my view on said issues;

- The NHS should not be privatized.
- Nursing Staff and Junior doctors should be on an above average salary, so as to be rewarded for the hard work they do.
- Our Military staff should be rewarded with an above average salary, as well as looked after fully following service for this great nation
- There should be no cuts made to mental health, addiction and recovery services, in fact more support should be given instead
- ALL education fees should be scrapped
- Scrap the Bedroom Tax Scheme
- Britain needs to stay in the EU
- We need to do more to get people onto the housing ladder, maybe 0% deposits and lower general prices on properties in need to some work and TLC, which someone who owned them would give.
- We need to introduce an immigration system based on what skills an individual can bring to our economy, just like other countries have done for years now successfully
- We need to introduce minimum unit pricing on alcohol
- We need to legalise Cannabis

So all these sorts of issues boil down to money. How can we generate the money to cover these costs and also help pay the debt we have agreed to pay for the bankers? There's a few ways;

- Freeze MP's salaries so they can not go any higher then they already are which is too high as it is. Ban any bonus for MP's and cap expenses at a reasonable level.
- Introduce Mansion Tax
- Ban all banker bonus and freeze banker salaries which again are far too high
- Force companies and celebrities to pay there due taxes

I remain just one thing, and one thing only, and that is a clown. It places me on a far higher plane than any politician - Charlie Chaplin

Naloxone

We're all in the same game, just different levels, dealing with the same hell, just different devils!

We are all angels with a damaged wing; only by standing with each other will we learn to fly again!

Naloxone saves lives, FACT! If there was something that could bring someone back from the brink of death from say a cardiac arrest or an epilepsy induced seizure or any other major trauma, it would be declared a 'miracle of modern medicine' Naloxone is no different!

Naloxone is a very commonly used competitive opioid antagonist. This means that it binds with the opioid receptors in the brain/body without activating them. To put it another way; naloxone is a medicine that can temporarily reverse the effect of an opioid by removing the opioid from the receptors, thereby assisting with the restoration of breathing. Naloxone has been used for many years by doctors and nurses in hospitals for reversal of post operative respiratory depression, and reversal of respiratory and Central Nervous System depression from opioid administration during labour and child birth. Naloxone is also used by paramedics in communities to reverse the effect of opioid overdose.

Naloxone does not get a person intoxicated/stoned/high, quite the opposite. Naloxone is not poisonous, and causes NO harm if swallowed. Naloxone is very safe, but does have some contraindications. Naloxone is a Prescription Only Medication and is currently only licensed in the UK for administration by subcutaneous, intramuscular or intravenous injection. In Scotland naloxone is also supplied to people under a Patient Group Direction (PGD). The PGD for supply of naloxone is a special document, agreed by senior clinician's, nurses and pharmacists so that they can legally supply the medicine to people who might be at risk of opioid related overdoses without first looking at the persons medical record or consulting a doctor, who would normally be responsible for writing a prescription. Naloxone comes in various presentations. In the UK naloxone comes in ampoules, pre-filled syringes and mini jets. It is manufactured in two different concentrations, 0.4mg per ml, and 1mg per ml. In Scotland it has been decided to use a 1mg per ml concentration that comes in a 2 ml pre filled syringe, meaning that people are supplied with 2mlg of the medication.

Amongst the reform I suggest, as I have written about in the previous chapter, I want to see Naloxone introduced into schools and youth facilities.

Furthermore I feel we need to look at the stigma and attitudes surrounding overdose incidents. By this I mean we need to introduce a system applicable to medical and law authorities where we practice a method of treatment, often life saving, first and questions later. I say this because I have heard of incidents not at all uncommon where if an ambulance is called for an overdose, the local police who have been informed of the incident, will show up to the scene before paramedics looking for a prosecution in waging the war on drugs. I have also heard stories of paramedics being shoved out the way and stopped from giving life saving treatment so that police can search the individual for drugs first. It seems only common sense to point out that life saving treatment is needed before any letter of law is applied, how are you going to prosecute someone if they die?

80% of Heroin users inject with a friend, which is weird, because 80% of overdose victims found by paramedics, are all alone

Gambling Taxes

The tax collector must love poor people; he is creating so many of them

The gambling industry in the United Kingdom is now worth in excess of £7 billion. Last year, the UK Gambling Commission (UKGC) revealed financial figures for the 12 months ending September 2014 which showed the UK gambling industry is worth £7.1 billion, not including the National Lottery.

The massive figure is an increase of £327 million (up 5%) when compared to April 2013 to March 2014.

Land based betting continues to be the most popular way for Brits to place wagers and accounted for 47% of the £7.1bn Gross Gambling Yield (GGY). The next largest betting medium was online sports betting (19%), followed by online casinos (16%), bingo (9%), arcades (5%) and social lotteries (5%). Of those six categories only bingo and arcade revenue saw a decrease. Gross Gambling Yield is the amount retained by operators after the payment of winnings but before the deduction of the costs of operation.

The UK now has in excess of 9000 betting shops employing a well over 50,000 people, with William Hill owning the most with over 2000 shops, closely followed by Ladbrokes then Gala Coral, Betfred and other operators making up the rest.

Of all the online gambling markets it is sports betting that generated the most revenue with £1.19bn worth, with 56% of this figure stemming from punters betting on the outcome of football matches. Total remote GGY weighed in at £1.371bn which would have generated income of £205.7m million had the 15% Point of Consumption Tax being in force.

With the increase in bookies on the high street, many online betting sites and the amount of advertising for gambling done on TV etc, as well as the amount of money generated by highly addictive FOB machines the virtual roulette and slot machines, gambling addiction in the UK is now as real an issue as addiction to substances and needs treating in equal measure to substance based addictions.

Here is what I want to campaign for in this section, if the UK government gave up just 1%, which lets be honest is nothing percentage wise, which in cash is £70 million, and invested that into supporting addiction and mental health services, recovery services and communities and ensured no cuts were made to pre-existing services, the difference it would make moving forward would be monumental.

For a nation to try to tax itself into prosperity is like a man standing in a bucket and trying to lift himself up by the handle –Winston Churchill

Alcohol Advertising

Drink does not drown Care, but waters it, and makes it grow faster - Benjamin Franklin

I want to change how alcohol is advertised, in particular in supermarkets. At any one time supermarkets usually have multiple bulk buy drink offers and in most of the stores the first thing you will see when you walk in the door is stacks of cheap beer on offer with an appealing sale point. Supermarkets are contributing to an epidemic of heavy drinking by promoting cheap alcohol that is poorly labeled. Alcohol Concern has been looking at how much information is available to the public about the unit content of the alcohol products they are buying. Looking at beer, wine and spirits that were heavily promoted by branches of five major supermarkets, they assessed the labels of the products for five key pieces of information; unit content, information on sensible drinking levels, guidance around drinking and pregnancy, the 'Know Your Limits' government message and the 'Drink aware' website.

This snap shot found that only 28 out of the 50 promoted products they looked at had unit information on the labels 56%. Equally as worrying, only 9 of the 50 promoted products displayed sensible drinking levels on the labels 18%. Only two promoted products 4% had all five elements suggested by the Department of Health. The public is currently being given insufficient information to be able to know how much they are drinking and what level of drinking is healthy.

Current legislation means that consumers are often given more content and health information if they drink a non-alcoholic beer, than if they drink a standard beer. Alcohol Concern believes that this disparity is totally at odds with the harms alcohol causes to individuals, families and communities. It is also at odds with the government's own agenda of promoting choice and providing information so that individuals can make healthy decisions about their lifestyles. The public has a right to know how much they are drinking and what levels of consumption are safe. A recent survey by Alcohol Concern found that 94.5% of 1,088 respondents agreed that prominent information about the total units per drink of alcohol should be displayed wherever alcohol is sold. Alcohol costs the UK economy more than £25 billion a year, with £2.5bn of that taken up with NHS costs.

Alcohol Concern also assessed the supermarkets own brand alcohol products. A huge 95% of own brand products had unit labeling but only 44% displayed sensible drinking levels. This clearly shows that supermarkets are aware that they have a responsibility to provide consumers with information yet their practice in promoting poorly labeled products is contrary to this knowledge. Consumers need information to make healthy choices about their consumption and supermarkets need to be more responsible in the way they promote alcohol. Drinks producers have failed to comply with the voluntary agreement they made with the government to improve their labeling. The government must now take firm action to help consumers understand how much alcohol is in what they are drinking and what the health consequences are if they drink too much.

I would recommend some of the following improvements;

•All pre-packaged alcoholic beverages should be required, by law, to display its unit content. This information must be accompanied with information about sensible drinking levels. These labels must be clearly in the field of vision, the numbers must be at least 3mm high and must be horizontal to the level of the product so that it can be easily read by consumers. This new standard must be mandated by the Food Standards Agency as the current voluntary agreement between the drinks industry and the government has been ineffective.

•All pre-packaged alcoholic products should include space for a government defined health warning. These messages would be similar to those on cigarette packages. Messages might include statements such as'; 'Drinking above sensible limits puts you at risk of throat, mouth and larynx cancer'. These messages would have to be determined by the Department of Health and would have to have a specified size and place on alcoholic products. Industry defined messages are insufficient. The phrase 'Please drink responsibly' is too general; offering no information about what responsible drinking actually is.

•As responsible retailer's supermarkets should not promote alcoholic products which do not have clear unit labeling; information about sensible drinking levels and a warning about drinking whilst pregnant or trying to conceive.

•Off-licenses, including supermarkets, should display information about what sensible drinking levels are and the health consequences of drinking to excess at any point where alcohol is displayed or for sale. This should be brought in through a Mandatory Code on Alcohol Sales.

•The government should look again at introducing a minimum price on alcohol as recommended by the Chief Medical Officer and as proposed by the Scottish Government. A minimum price of 50p per unit would eliminate some of the most irresponsible promotions as well as having a significant impact in reducing alcohol related hospital admissions, crime and work absenteeism.

•The promotion and sale of alcohol should be confined to one specific aisle in supermarkets and not spread throughout the whole store, especially as a sale point at the very front of the store, at till points or alongside pre made meals as to suggest that alcohol is required to consume the food.

I can think of one supermarket in particular that advertise regularly on TV weekend deals where you can buy a 2 or 3 course meals for two people and a drink, which is alcohol, why can't this include a soft drink instead? Why does it have to be alcohol?

When life gets you down, do you wanna know what you've got to do, just keep swimming – Finding Nemo

Minimum Unit Pricing

Drunkenness is nothing but voluntary madness – Seneca

Oh yes Alcohol, the old devil juice! A poison we happily pour down our necks! Scientific tests have proven Alcohol more harmful then Heroin, Crack and Meth yet it's fully legal to buy 24 hours on a day on every street corner in the land. If Alcohol was invented a new today, it would be a Class A drug. FACT if you do not drink now day and age, you are seen as alien by the majority of people, these are strange times we live in! – Karl Newton

Alcohol Concern has been working tirelessly to try and introduce minimum unit pricing for alcoholic drinks. They believe that the minimum unit price for alcohol should be at least 50p.

Minimum pricing would mean that there is a baseline price for alcohol, below which it couldn't be sold. This campaign targets high strength alcoholic drinks that is sold very cheaply, drinks that are often consumed by the heaviest drinkers, as well as by younger drinkers. Moderate drinkers will feel little effect from minimum pricing. Alcohol related harm remains one of the biggest health problems facing the UK, with over 10 million adults drinking more than recommended guidelines. Alcohol is a contributor to 60 different diseases and its excessive consumption is a significant cause of premature death in the UK. It costs the NHS £3.5 billion, while alcohol related crime costs an estimated £11 billion each year.

Approximately 2.6 million children in the UK are living with parents who are drinking dangerous amounts, while over 700,000 live with dependent drinkers. There is a clear link between the price of alcohol and the level of alcohol related harm, so it goes without saying that the most effective way to reduce harm is to control price and availability.

In 2012, the government committed to introducing a minimum unit price for alcohol. Later that year, the Home Office released a consultation recommending a minimum unit price of 45p. Along with many other organisations, Alcohol Concern is calling for a minimum unit price of 50p, as this will have a greater impact on reducing alcohol-related harm. It will also be in line with what has happened in Scotland where legislation has already been passed.

Using a model from Sheffield University the Government Consultation states that the 45p minimum price will reduce alcohol consumption by 4.3%, saving 2,000 lives and 66,000 hospital admissions after 10 years. There will also be curbs on multi-buys and much promotional activity, justified by the need to reduce binge drinking and public order problems in town centres at the weekend. This policy is backed by the Alcohol Health Alliance, an umbrella organisation of 32 medical and counselling organisations, as well as by CAMRA, the real ale organisation and Greene King the brewer and pub chain.

Dr. Sarah Wollaston MP. Dr Sarah Wollaston MP was elected Member of Parliament for Totnes in May 2010 and lives in South Devon with her husband Adrian and three children. Previously a GP, then police forensic examiner and finally a teacher of junior doctors; Sarah first entered politics through the first open primary and has sought to bring 'real life' experience to politics. Sarah was spurred into Politics by her opposition to the threatened closure of Moretonhampstead Community Hospital.

Sarah was voted onto the Health Select Committee in the summer of 2010 and has continued to speak out about the NHS reforms. Sarah continues to speak out about the cost of alcohol.

On the matter of minimum unit pricing Sarah says; most people will know someone whose life has been ruined through being unable to control their drinking. If they were the only one to suffer then this might be a matter of personal choice and responsibility.

The fact is that problem drinking leaves a trail of destruction in its wake.

Around half of violent crime including homicide and domestic violence is attributable to or aggravated by alcohol and over 700,000 children live with an alcoholic parent. Our casualty departments are overflowing and over a million people are admitted to hospital annually as a result.

If the problem is serious enough, and a conservative estimate puts the cost to our economy and to individuals at around £20billion per year, then Government has a duty to do something more than hand wringing. The costs are hard to quantify as official figures don't account for disasters like the lifetime care of a child born with foetal alcohol syndrome or the fallout from a fatal crash caused by a drunk driver.

The evidence is clear that the 3 areas that would make the most difference in reducing the carnage are price, availability and marketing.

I wouldn't suggest for a minute that price alone could cure our national drinking problem but without addressing the availability day and night of ultra cheap alcohol from virtually every street corner, the other measures would not be effective. As a psychoactive, addictive carcinogen we should stop treating alcohol as an ordinary commodity.

I'm backing minimum pricing because it works and would save lives without hitting those on low incomes. At present, pricing and taxation bear little relation to the amount of alcohol in a drink and supermarkets are free to offer alcohol as a loss leader which is subsidised by raising the price on non alcohol products. Without a minimum price they would continue to do so.

We know that pricing influences demand and that the heaviest drinkers pay on average 40% less per unit than moderate consumers for their alcohol. In particular young binge drinkers target cheaper alcohol promotions. The ban on cheap multibuys has already reduced demand in Scotland and it is a shame that some supermarkets have tried to undermine this by offering cheap deliveries from South of the border.

So if a minimum price were introduced would that harm low income moderate drinkers? It depends on the level at which it is set. Would 45p per unit, as proposed in Scotland really be damaging? In practice a bottle of wine with between 9 and 11 units would work out at costing at least £4.50 and a 2unit pint of lager at least 90p.

Currently cheap supermarket alcohol, routinely available at 17p per unit, means that a teenage girl can be drunk for 68p. At 45p per unit this becomes less attractive and price does influence demand in teenage drinkers.

Low income moderate drinkers are already subsidising the supermarket promotions but they face a double whammy as low income areas also bear the brunt of alcohol related crime and antisocial behavior.

There is no point at all in an alcohol strategy unless it is evidence based with a good chance of making a difference. There is no such thing as a cheap drink; we are all paying a heavy price.

Philip Davies MP. Philip graduated from the University of Huddersfield with an Upper Second honors degree in Historical and Political Studies and before being elected, Philip worked for Asda for 12 years, working his way up from the bottom to be a Senior Marketing Manager. Philip was elected to parliament for Shipley in 2005 with a majority of 422 and was re-elected as the MP for Shipley in 2010 with a majority of 9,944. He was also elected onto the Executive Committee of the 1922 Committee of backbench Conservative MPs in 2006 and has been re-elected back onto it every year since. He has also served on the Culture, Media and Sports Select Committee since 2006. Philip is also a member of the newly established Backbench Business Committee and is on the panel of Chairmen for Westminster Hall Debates and the Committee stage of Bills. Philip became the first MP to publicly call for Britain to withdraw from the European Union and is a member of The Freedom Association's 'Better Off Out' campaign. He is also the Parliamentary Spokesman for the Campaign Against Political Correctness. In 2011, Philip won an award at the Spectator Parliamentary Awards as Readers Representative of the Year.

On minimum unit pricing Philip says; the very principle of minimum pricing goes against all my beliefs as a libertarian and believer in individual freedom and responsibility. Undoubtedly, there are a small percentage of society who suffer from alcohol related problems including binge drinking and anti-social behavior. However, to punish the vast majority of responsible drinkers for the actions of a troublesome few by hiking up alcohol prices across the board is at worst completely unfair and at best, downright perverse.

The people who would be most penalised by minimum pricing are those who are already on tight budgets, such as pensioners, people on fixed incomes or those in low-paid jobs. I simply cannot understand the logic, at a time of economic austerity, how anyone can justify imposing further artificial price rises, deliberately targeted at the very poorest in society.

The Institute for Fiscal Studies produced a report on minimum pricing that found that poorer households, compared with richer households, on average pay less for a unit of off-sale alcohol. For example, households with an income of less than £10,000 a year pay 39.8p per unit, while those on a household income of more than £70,000 pay 49.3p per unit on average. As a result, a minimum price of 40p or 45p per unit would have a larger impact on poorer households and virtually no impact on richer ones.

In addition, the process of setting a minimum price is predicated on the assumption that raising the price of alcohol will make those who misuse alcohol behave differently. However, that is an incredibly simplistic belief.

In fact all of the evidence shows that alcohol pricing has little impact on the habits of heavy drinkers. It's surely obvious, that those who like to drink to excess are the least likely to be deterred from drinking by price rises. We know that thanks to above inflation increases in excise duty for several years, the UK already has some of the highest priced alcohol in Europe, and yet there is no evidence to support the notion that these high prices have deterred alcohol misuse. In fact it's the high tax/high price countries like Sweden and the UK that tend to have a problem with alcohol misuse whereas low tax/low price Spain and Italy do not.

All of which suggests that minimum unit pricing wouldn't work to combat the real issues of binge drinking and alcohol misuse which we all agree is the problem, but is very likely to reduce the intake of responsible drinkers. If wine suddenly jumps from £5 to £10 a bottle then clearly some people will buy less. But this doesn't mean that alcohol misuse by an undeterred minority is going to be lowered.

To date, in the UK overall consumption has fallen by 11% since 2004, but reported levels of alcohol harm continue to rise. Nevertheless, health professionals continue to push for the imposition of prices rises, despite this lack of evidence and despite the fact that a minimum unit price has never been successfully imposed on a national level anywhere in the world.

So if blanket price increases are not the answer, what is? Other methods have had far more obvious success in tackling binge drinkers. We know from experience elsewhere that targeted interventions at problem drinkers have far more impact than taxation increases. So rather than thrashing out with an illiberal, anti-Government, nanny state approach, we should focus our efforts where they will make a difference. Rather than hitting everyone with a price increase, let's target those people that misuse alcohol, let's enforce existing laws about public drunkenness and punish those responsible for anti-social behavior. Let's support schemes like Drinkaware and Community Alcohol Partnerships which seek to use education to tackle problems such as underage drinking. Surely it is better that we look to combat alcohol abuse at the cultural, psychological and behavioural root of the problem, rather than impose a blanket regressive price hike on the decent, hard working, law abiding majority for whom a pint of beer, a glass of wine, or a dram of whisky, is one of the few pleasures in their hard working week!

Finally, I worry where this will end. Will the Government suggest later down the line that we should introduce minimum pricing of cream cakes, pizzas, chocolate, fish and chips or curry, because they are all bad for us if eaten to excess? This is a slippery slope, and certainly not one that I am prepared to support.

Both those opinions were shared by the MP's on the Centre for Policy Studies website, www.cps.org.uk

I am fully in favor of introducing a minium unit price of 50p given the proven effect doing so has had north of the border in Scotland.

Determine that the thing can and shall be done, and then we shall find the way – Abraham Lincoln

Mindfulness

Mindfulness helps you go home to the present. And every time you go there and recognise a condition of happiness that you have, happiness comes - Nhat Hanh

Mindfulness is a practice with roots reaching as far back as the ancient traditions of Buddhist meditation. However, mindfulness has assumed a much more secular role in our society today. Mindfulness has been scientifically proven to reveal important health benefits, and it is practiced in many different forms, including traditional meditation. Mindfulness is essentially awareness. It is the practice of sustaining awareness of our thoughts, feelings, physical sensations, and external environment in the present moment. Contrary to popular belief, mindfulness is not about trying to attain some sort of nirvana or enlightened state. It is exactly the opposite: accepting and existing in the present, whatever that present looks like.

Mindfulness is a simple form of meditation that was little known about in the west until recent years. A typical meditation consists of focusing your full attention on your breath as it flows in and out of your body. Focusing on each breath in a way which allows you to observe your thoughts as they arise in your mind and, little by little, to let go of struggling with them. You come to realise that thoughts come and go of their own accord; that you are not your thoughts. You can watch as they appear in your mind, seemingly from thin air, and watch again as they disappear, like a soap bubble bursting. You come to the profound understanding that thoughts and feelings including negative ones are transient. They come and they go, and ultimately, you have a choice about whether to act on them or not. Another way of describing it is like staring at a stream running by with leafs floating on it. The stream flows toward you, bringing your thoughts with it which leap off the leafs like frogs, into your hand. You acknowledge the frog but ultimately place it back on the leaf and allow it to be carried away on its natural course by the flow of the stream.

Mindfulness is about observation without criticism, being compassionate with yourself. When unhappiness or stress hover overhead, rather than taking it all personally, you learn to treat them as if they were black clouds in the sky, and to observe them with friendly curiosity as they drift past. In essence, mindfulness allows you to catch negative thought patterns before they tip you into a downward spiral. It begins the process of putting you back in control of your life and offers you essential tools to manage your mind in times of stress.

Over time, mindfulness brings about long term changes in mood and levels of happiness and wellbeing. Scientific studies have shown that mindfulness not only prevents depression, but that it also positively affects the brain patterns underlying day-to-day anxiety, stress, depression and irritability so that when they arise, they dissolve away again more easily.

While many people think mindfulness and meditation are the same thing, they are actually quite different. Meditation is traditional meditation typically involving sitting, relaxed but attentive with your eyes closed, in a quiet place conducive to peacefulness.

Mindfulness is the practice of awareness in itself. This means it can be performed anywhere at any time.

Research has shown that people who have had three or more episodes of depression have a high risk of becoming depressed again; however, this risk can be reduced if antidepressants are taken for 2 years after recovery or if patients attend a course of mindfulness-based cognitive therapy (MBCT).

The PREVENT trial was designed to find out if over 24 months MBCT with support to taper/stop antidepressants (MBCT-TS) reduced the number of relapses/recurrences compared with continuing antidepressants for patients who had experienced three or more previous episodes of depression. In total, 424 people took part and half were randomly allocated to attend an MBCT-TS course and stop taking antidepressants and half were allocated to stay on their antidepressants.

The results suggest that MBCT-TS is not better than antidepressants at preventing depression recurring; at the end of the 24-month period the number of people who had become depressed again was very similar in both groups (MBCT-TS 44%, antidepressants 47%). It would seem that both treatments were relatively effective at keeping people well. It did not find a difference between the two treatments in terms of cost.

However, it did find that for people who are at a higher risk of relapse/recurrence MBCT-TS may in fact be more effective than antidepressants and further research has been recommended to explore this relationship in more depth.

I would like to see the introduction of more mindfulness based therapy's rather then prescriptions to medicines. Furthermore I would like to see mindfulness introduced into educational teachings to give the next generation a set of tools and coping mechanisms against the strains of day to day life, to try and prevent substance use or violence or even self harm instead.

Respond; don't react. Listen; don't talk. Think; don't assume - Raji Lukkoor

Recovery Communities & Hubs

There is a place in this movement for everybody, whether you just want to share your story at a school, share your story with your neighbor or you want to speak to your legislator about how important supporting addiction recovery is for our communities - Greg Williams

Recovery communities aim to provide an individual with all the local services they need to sustain abstinence including providing help with housing, career and peer and health support so that the individual can continue to make lasting changes to improve their quality of life. Recovery community organisations are at the heart and soul of the recovery movement. They are major hubs for recovery focused policy advocacy activities, carrying out recovery focused community education and outreach programs, and becoming players in system change initiatives. Many are also providing peer based recovery support services. Recovery communities share a recovery vision, authenticity of voice and are independent, serving as a bridge between diverse communities of recovery, the addiction treatment community, governmental agencies, the criminal justice system, the larger network of health and human service providers and systems and the broader recovery support resources of the extended community.

Recovery communities and hubs are vital and I see them very much as the future of recovery within the UK and in fact worldwide. I feel it should be seen as a minimum requirement to have at least 1 recovery community or hub per county in the UK. In fact I would go as far as to say that, that alone is not good enough either, we need to aim to have a recovery community in each major town or city throughout the United Kingdom. This should be seen as a minimum requirement to aid people in their recovery and should be supported by all means possible by the UK government.

There are multiple pathways of addiction recovery and ALL are cause for celebration! - William L. White

Homelessness in the UK

There is a lot that happens around the world we cannot control. We cannot stop earthquakes, we cannot prevent droughts, and we cannot prevent all conflict, but when we know where the hungry, the homeless and the sick exist, then we can help - Jan Schakowsky

In 2015 Government statistics showed that 3,569 people slept rough on any one night across England - this is over double the number counted in 2010. Local agencies report 7,581 people slept rough in London alone throughout 2014/15 - A 16% rise on the previous year, and more than double the figure of 3,673 in 2009/10.

Homelessness simply shouldn't exist in this day and age. It belongs to another era – a Dickensian time when extreme poverty forced people to take desperate measures just to survive. Nevertheless, in the last year alone, the number of people sleeping rough on England's streets soared by nearly a third, and now stands at more than double what it was in 2010.

Homelessness isn't inevitable, and we don't need to look very far to find an alternative. As the situation in England reaches crisis proportions, Wales is undergoing a quiet revolution in the way it tackles homelessness, driven largely by legislation that has changed the way help is offered to homeless people.

At 'Crisis' they have long been calling for similarly bold action to change the law in England. While the recent budget announced that £110m would be directed towards helping people off the streets and out of hostels, we cannot tackle homelessness with money alone, and that is where the approach of the Welsh government comes in.

In 2015, Wales enacted a new law requiring councils to help prevent people from becoming homeless, and while it isn't perfect, they're already having considerable success. According to the latest figures for Wales, where councils intervened to prevent people from becoming homeless in the first place, they were successful in two thirds of cases. Alongside that, they have seen a drop of two thirds in the number of people formally accepted as homeless.

The situation in Wales is still in flux, but the early signs are positive. Meanwhile in England, the case for change is overwhelming. As it stands, the law in England means that single homeless people who go to their councils for help can be turned away to sleep on the streets often cold, desperate and forgotten. This is unacceptable, and it needs to stop.

If the government is serious about tackling homelessness, we need a change in the law so that all homeless people can get the help they need. With all forms of homelessness on the rise, now is the time for action. The government has already made a commitment to consider options, including legislation, to prevent more people from becoming homeless, and I strongly urge them to follow through on this. Nobody should be forced to sleep rough because they can't get the help they need.

We have a huge task ahead of us, and many of the underlying causes remain: more and more people are struggling to pay their rent in an increasingly insecure market, while cuts to housing benefit and local council funding have left the safety net in tatters. A change in the law certainly isn't a cure-all, and councils will need the funding to make it work, but it will put England on a much better track than the one it's on now.

Homelessness isn't inevitable. We're already seeing significant improvements in Wales, while in Scotland there is talk about the possibility of ending homelessness within a generation. Homelessness belongs in the past, but now we need bold, decisive action to send it there.

In recent times, the body of 23 year-old Daniel Smith was found in a burning tent in Manchester. The same day, 32 year-old Christopher Sever was found dead in a derelict house in Hull. Two weeks before that, a 50 year-old man's body was discovered in a car park in Swindon. Three tragic deaths in the space of a fortnight, each from different causes but with one thing in common: they were all homeless.

With homelessness in the UK soaring, deaths like these will inevitably become more common. According to the charity Crisis, the average life expectancy of a homeless person is just 47 and they are 13 times more likely to be victims of violence.

Since 2010, rough sleeping in England has increased by 55% and last year saw a surge in homeless camps being set up around the country. When local councils are challenged about the camps, the stock response is usually that occupants were offered accommodation but turned it down. What they fail to say is the offer was usually just a bed in a shelter for a couple of nights rather than a permanent solution.

Many local authorities have resorted to controversial ways of trying to keep the problem out of sight. Some have sought to prosecute those found sleeping rough or begging, while others have deployed increasingly invasive tactics to keep rough sleepers off the streets - from 'anti-homeless spikes' to water hoses, to loudspeakers installed to prevent homeless people from sleeping. But, what, if anything, is actually being done to prevent or tackle the issue, rather than just attempting to keep it from view?

We need to change our attitudes towards homeless people as well. The first thing I always practice is that instead of giving someone on the street struggling and begging a hand out of some kind, we should instead take 5/10 minutes out of our day to show some compassion and sit down and talk to them, see if there is anyway we can help them. Secondly I never give money to people begging, it can all too often be mis-used, I always instead buy the person asking some food and a hot beverage.

Bleak, dark, and piercing cold, it was a night for the well-housed and fed to draw round the bright fire, and thank God they were at home; and for the homeless starving wretch to lay him down and die. Many hunger-worn outcasts close their eyes in our bare streets at such times, who, let their crimes have been what they may, can hardly open them in a more bitter world - Charles Dickens, Oliver Twist

New drink driving prevention invention
Drinking and driving is a gamble that you just can't win

In 2013, provisional figures show that 260 people were killed, 1,110 were seriously injured and there were over 8,000 casualties in total in drink drive accidents. Although the level of drinking and driving has dropped dramatically over the last three decades, over 250 people are still killed in drink drive accidents every year (about 1 in 6 of all road deaths). Despite 30 years of drink drive education and enforcement, over 70,000 people are still caught drink driving annually.

Often it is an innocent person who suffers, not the driver who is over the drink drive limit. In 2012, 80 pedestrians were killed or seriously injured by drink drivers, as were 30 motorcyclists and 360 car passengers. 50 children were killed or seriously injured by drink drivers that year. In 2013, 683,651 roadside breath tests were carried out by the police, which 71,675 drivers or riders (12% of those tested) failed or refused to take the test. Clearly, there is still much to do to prevent drink drive accidents, deaths and injuries.

According to drinkdriving.org website, roughly 90,000 people are convicted of drink driving each year in the United Kingdom. On average a further 3,000 people are killed or seriously injured each year in drink and driving collisions. One way I think we can address this issue is with a new invention idea I have come up with using the latest in technology. Most cars now have a key fob where you press a button to open it, I feel we should add a breathalyzer onto this as well. It will then give you a simple yes or no answer as to whether or not you are over the limit and if you are the car will not open. If then the car is opened and the engine activated within a period relative to how long it would take for your alcohol blood level to come back down to within the limit, it would automatically send the initial reading and a GPS location to traffic police who can then track the car down and take the relevant checks and action. It might be as simple as a sober friend instead is driving and the police allow them to continue as long as insurance and license is all correct etc. On the other hand, it could however be that the individual over the limit has got someone else to do a fraudulent blow to open the car and then drove anyway and the police would need to take further action.

Alcohol Ignition Interlock Devices (Alcolocks) Some countries require Breath Alcohol Ignition Interlock devices to be fitted to convicted offenders vehicles. They are designed to prevent a car engine from starting if the person who breathes into the device has been drinking alcohol. There is some evidence that they are effective in discouraging re-offending while the order is in force, but that re-offending occurs once the restriction is removed.

A small trial of an alcohol ignition interlock programme in Britain in which alcolocks were fitted to the vehicles of convicted drink drive offenders found that almost half (43%) of the participants failed to complete the 12 months programme. However, the devices did detect, and therefore, prevent many occasions in which a participant tried to start their car with alcohol in their system, including 328 occasions when the level of alcohol was above the drink drive limit.

The main problems reported by participants included being over the interlock limit the morning after drinking, delay in starting the car due to the time taken for the interlock to warm-up, and difficulties with rolling re-tests during a journey. Many of the participants indicated that the devices made them at least think seriously about their drinking, if not help change their drinking patterns outright

By drinking and driving, you risk your life, those of your passengers and others on the road.

www.ingramcontent.com/pod-product-compliance
Lightning Source LLC
Chambersburg PA
CBHW081541280526
45788CB00010B/3314